BETWEEN
HEAVEN
AND
EARTH

Poems by

William Marr

PublishAmerica
Baltimore

First printing

PublishAmerica has allowed this work to remain exactly as the author intended, verbatim, without editorial input.

Hardcover 978-1-4512-9089-9
Softcover 978-1-4512-9090-5
PUBLISHED BY PUBLISHAMERICA, LLLP
www.publishamerica.com
Baltimore

Printed in the United States of America

Acknowledgments

Four Seasons, Breath, and On the Towpath, JOURNAL OF LITERATURE & AESTHETICS; A Mosquito's Ode to a Toad, AUST CAI HONG YING (Australia); A Fallen Goddess, THE CHINESE POETRY INTERNATIONAL (China); Aftershock, THE CHINESE PEN (Taiwan); Mona Lisa, Neighbor's Flowers, NEW WORLD POETRY; The Cove, Transmigration, DUPAGE ARTS LIFE; Bridge, KAVYAM (an international literary journal, India); Katrina, BEYONG KATRINA, Ed. Patricia Ellyn Powell, Arts & Healthcare Press; Anxiety, A Tree Under The Morning Sun, Masquerade, Lake Louise, Social Event, Christmas Eve, A Dark Horse, Gravity, At the Laundromat, A Butterfly Specimen, Sea O Sea, ILLINOIS STATE POETRY SOCIETY WEBSITE ; Television, The Homesick Drunk, Typhoon Season, Drinking Tea at a Family Reunion, Story, Autumn Leaves, SELECTED POEMS OF WILLIAM MARR, The World Contemporary Poetry Series, The Milky Way Publishing Co. (Hong Kong); Bird Cage, Inflation, The Thinker, Reading, Autumn Window, Yellow River, Chicago Serenade, Chicago Serenade, Portrait, Kissing, El Nino, Morning Web, White House Sex Scandal, RED FROG—POEMS FROM THE PLANET EARTH (an online poetry journal, English/ Hebrew); Sharing an Umbrella, A Leap Second, Clone Songs, A Dreamless Night, Temple, PEGASUS, Fall/Winter Issue, Kentucky State Poetry Society; On the Treacherous Night Sea, Necktie, Spring, A Midsummer Day's Dream, Two Suns or More, Melting Icicles, Have a Hammock, POETRY SKY (an online poetry journal, Chinese/English); Memorial Day, ANTHOLOGY OF POETS AGAINST THE WAR, edited by Sam Hamill; African Boy, Extraterrestrials, Retirement, A Drunk World, Biltmore Mansion, Cezanne's Still Life, CHINESE-WESTERN POETRY (China); Vietnam War Memorial, Installation Art, Song of Birth and Death, GOING 60 IN CHICAGO, Ed. Eloise Bradley Fink, Thorntree Press; Dandelion, TAIWAN POETRY QUARTERLY; A Star-Studded World, COLOURS OF THE HEART (Noble House, London); Canadian Rockies' Pines, Jade Necklace, Bird Fish Poet, POETRY NETWORK (Hong Kong); Deer-Xing, The Moonless Moon Festival, Between Heaven and Earth, PRAIRIE LIGHT REVIEW; Eclipse, FROST AT MIDNIGHT, The National Library of Poetry; Ghost Story, Scent, The Transmigration of a Humorist, HEARTPLACE (an online poetry journal); Television, Bird Cage, OCARINA'S, ANTHOLOGY OF INTERNATIONAL CREATIVE POETRY; Composition, ANTHOLOGY ON WORLD BROTHERHOOD AND PEACE edited by Amado M.Yuzon, Parnassus Publications, Manila ; Picasso Died This Morning, OCARINA'S ANTHOLOGY OF AMERICAN AND WORLD POETRY 1978-79 Madras, India and RHYTHM AND RHYME (New Zealand); Fairy Penguin Parade, CHRISTIAN SCIENCE MONITOR.

Contents

I.
From
AUTUMN WINDOW

Sharing an Umbrella 15
Dandelion 16
Bird Cage 17
Mountain 18
Necktie 19
Kissing 20
The Thinker 21
Reading 22
Story 23
A Post-It Note 24
Tree 25
A Flower Dropping Its Petals 26
Yellow River 27
Drinking Tea at a Family Reunion 28
Terraced Paddies 29
The Homesick Drunk 30
Watching Snow 31
Hopscotch 32
Chicago Serenade 33
Every Time I See… 34
Floating Flowers 35
This Morning's Sunshine Was So Wonderful 36
Dialogue 37
Watching the Ocean in San Francisco
    With a Former Red Guard 38

Portrait 39
Picasso Died This Morning 40
African Boy 41
Television 42
Extraterrestrials 43
On the Treacherous Night Sea 44
Memorial Day 45
Vietnam War Memorial 46
Inflation 47
Performers 48
Road 49
Under the Night Sky 50
Composition 51
Old Woman 52
Spring Thunder 53
Typhoon Season 54
Fall 55
Autumn Leaves 56
Autumn Window 57
Spring 58
Summer 59

II.
Beyond
AUTUMN WINDOW

Song of Birth and Death 63
The Tree Under the Morning Sun 64
Trees 65
Go-Go Dance 66
Midnight Mass 67
Anxiety 68

Autumn 69
Evening Smokestack 70
A Woman 71
Menarche 72
A Star-Studded World 73
Spring 74
Confucius Temple in Nanjing 75
Masquerade 76
April Fool's Day 77
Canadian Rockies 78
Lake Louise 79
Athabasca Falls 80
Deer X-ing 81
Silence 82
Eclipse 83
A Leap Second 84
Social Event 85
Ghost Story 86
Winter Andante 87
Retirement 88
Born to Smile 89
Mirror Lake 90
Sky Burial 91
Christmas Eve 93
Installation Art 94
Clone Songs 96
Spring Snow 98
A Dreamless Night 99
Temple 100
A Midsummer Day's Dream 101
The Moonless Moon Festival 102
A Dark Horse 103

El Nino 104
Morning Web 105
White House Sex Scandal 106
Gravity 107
Four Seasons 108
A Dry Quiescent Afternoon 110
Scent 111
The Game of Blocks 112
Carrying No Map, I Travel 113
A Mosquito's Ode to a Toad 114
The Four-Sided Buddhist Idol in Macao 115
A Fallen Goddess 116
Two Suns or More 117
Smokestack 118
Between Heaven and Earth 119
A Drunk World 120
Aftershock 121
Cherokee Casino 122
Biltmore Mansion 123
Cow & Cowhide 125
Mona Lisa 126
Cezanne's Still Life 127
Breath 128
Spring Itch 129
Super Lightspeed 130
Time Difference 131
On the Towpath 132
Bian-Zhong 133
On the Viewing Stand of Tian An Men 134
911 135
The Cove 136
Bridge 137

Night Cruise on River Tuo 138
Jade Necklace 139
Listening to a Childhood Song 140
Neighbor's Flowers 141
Transmigration 142
Songs of You and Me 143
Someone Must Be Crying 145
Tsunami Time 147
Melting Icicles 148
At the Laundromat 149
Have a Hammock 150
Newborn 151
Bird Fish Poet 152
Katrina 153
Endangered Species 154
An Easter Surprise 155
Jewish Cemetery in Budapest 156
A Helicopter Upside Down in a Public Place 157
The Transmigration of a Humorist 158
Winter Palaces Summer Palaces 159
Big Palaces Small Palaces 159
Toilet Reality 160
Mountain Views 161
A Butterfly Specimen 163
Fairy Penguin Parade 164
Recollection Tricks 166
Curves 167
Sea O Sea 168
Sydney Opera House 169
Snowstorm 170
About the Author 171

I.
From
AUTUMN WINDOW

Sharing an Umbrella

Sharing an umbrella
I suddenly realize the difference between us

Yet bending over to kiss you
give me such joy
as you try to meet me halfway
on tiptoe

Dandelion

The horizon is so far away
that the dandelion makes its roaming dream
a relay event

from
generation
to
generation

Bird Cage

open
the
cage
let the bird fly

away

give
freedom back
to the
bird
cage

Mountain

It's still there
for me to
climb

Looming from my childhood
my father's
back

Necktie

Before the mirror
he carefully makes himself
a tight knot

to let the hairy hand
of civilization
drag him
on

Kissing

It makes no difference
your lips kissing my lips
or my lips kissing yours

What is important
is that we still have something to say
to each other
and try to say it
well

The Thinker

Holding his chin
thinking
how to
hold the chin
and watch the computer
do
the thinking

Reading

Upon opening the book
words lead the way
sentences follow
All disappear in a flash

Only the best-selling title
and the hot name
of the author
remain
What a great book

Story

The dog has her eyes closed
but the old man knows she's listening

Her warm back is moving
closer and closer

A Post-It Note

I've put some
poems
in the icebox

They'll be cold
and sweet
when you get home

Tree

Day and night
I hear
the annual rings
inside my heart
rumbling
and wheeling
on the rugged road
toward the sky

A Flower Dropping Its Petals

Never
can I listen calmly
to you counting

forget me
forget me not
forget me
forget me not...

to the last petal

Yellow River

If you trace up the turbid current, you will find
as any geography book can tell you
the Kunlun Mountains in Qinghai

Yet according to history's bloody accounts
this river
which turns clear at most
once in a thousand years
has its origin in millions of eye sockets
of suffering human beings

Drinking Tea at a Family Reunion

After Thirty Long Years of Separation

Down at one gulp
how unbearable it would have been
to taste drop by drop
the cup of thirty bitter years

You smile and say to me
good tea
should be sipped
and savored

Terraced Paddies

Toiling hard
to build green-carpeted stairs
on a steep slope
for the heaven-ascending gods
to step on

The Homesick Drunk

He has walked a short alley
into a tortuous
writhing intestine
of ten thousand miles

One step left
ten years
one step right
ten years
O Mother
I am struggling
toward
you

Watching Snow

1

As the footprints in the snow
get deeper and deeper
they become harder and harder
to comprehend

2

Falling on the feverish face of
a homesick boy
the snow melts and turns into
a warm tropical shower

3

A sudden toll
of the steeple bell
shakes down
the snow
from the Cross

Hopscotch

Standing in the way
of a bullet's joyflight
another little girl fell
on a blood-stained pavement

A triumphant smile
crossed her twisted face
as she finally managed
to plant both feet
neatly
in the chalked squares

Chicago Serenade

Evening
a desolate street

A car with its windows tightly rolled up
stops for the red lights

Suddenly
in the rear-view mirror
a dark figure
looming

Sir, buy…

The ashen driver
steps in fright on the pedal
and rushes through the red lights
like a rabbit running for its life

…buy some flowers
today's Valentine's Day

Every Time I See...

Every time I see a little tree
budding timidly
in the spring breeze
I have an urge
to hold your thin shoulders in my arms
and squeeze

a good morning to you

Floating Flowers

On my front lawn
a swarm of butterflies
is busy dress-rehearsing
a midsummer day's dream

But merrily chasing each other in mid-air
the two in bright yellow
are in no hurry to come down
and take their places

This Morning's Sunshine Was So Wonderful

I set up the easel
enthusiastically started my painting

As soon as I finished covering the canvas with blue sky
a bird flew into the scene
I said, good, good, you came at the right time
please move up a little. Yes, that's it!
Then a green tree rose from the lower left corner
just in time to meet a passing white cloud
and the squirrels chasing each other
were not hard to catch
Soon I had a presentable painting at hand

Yet I felt something was missing
something deep and inharmonious
to bring out its purity and innocence

As I was busily mixing
some harsh and bleak color
a lonesome old man staggered into the picture
and finished my masterwork
with a blank stare

Dialogue

What are you running away from, old woman?
ARMY!
What kind of army? Red army or white army?
ARMY!

What are you hiding from, young mother?
BOMBS!
Which way are the bombs from? East or west?
BOMBS!

What are you crying about, little girl?
BLOOD!
Whose blood? Human or animal?
BLOOD!

Watching the Ocean in San Francisco With a Former Red Guard

Another wave rushed in
As I was about to ask
"Did you think of poetry in those days?"
it crashed on the black rocks
and retreated with a white sigh

We looked away at the bay
through a thick fog
Suddenly the sun appeared
brilliant and solemn
as if it were a miracle

but we both knew
it was there all the time

Portrait

They kept enlarging
his image
until its every pore
became a great
hollow

But before it could be put into the big frame
of history
Time, the critical old man
already started the work
of reduction
step by step
as he walked backward
squinting at it from a distance

Picasso Died This Morning

After frittering away the remaining afternoon
I walk up to the window many times
to see if the sky holds any last surprise

As it hangs over my neighbor's roof
the sun seems almost
immortal. Picasso died this morning
I wonder what tunes the three musicians
are going to play
which way the dove
is going to fly

Having shown us the world is still
soft and kneadable
the master hands are now withdrawing
I reach out unconsciously
but realizing how childish it must be
I turn my grasping hands to clapping

African Boy

Day and night
a monstrous stomach
wriggles in his bloated belly

sucking up
the unblossomed laughter
sucking up
the teardrops that moisten a mother's heart
sucking up
the meager flesh under his wrinkled skin
sucking up
the indifference in his eyes
and eventually sucking up
from his open mouth a ghastly cry
which we take for soundless
but is in fact at a pitch
well beyond the limit
of our comprehension

Television

The world
is easily
switched off

yet not quite

A spark of hatred
from the dimming screen
suddenly bursts into flames
soon spreading
over Vietnam
over the Middle East
over every feverish face

Extraterrestrials

The evening newscast
is swarming with images
of extraterrestrials

Protruding foreheads
dark and skinny
and big eyes
staring straight out
from sunken sockets

What?
Starving Africans?
no wonder they look
so familiar

On the Treacherous Night Sea

a broken refugee boat appears
like a ghost
on the tired sleepless eyelids
jolting and rolling
toward the ever-narrowing harbor
of humanity
toward the shore
where lights die out
one after another

Memorial Day

At Arlington, someone
Unknown goes down

The thousands, the thousands
Who have gone down in faraway fields
But who won't die in the heart—
How do we bury
The thousands

Vietnam War Memorial

A block of marble
and twenty six letters of the alphabet
etch so many young names
onto history

Wandering alone
amid the mass grave
an old woman has at last found
her only child
and with her eyes tightly shut
her trembling fingers now feel
for the mortal wound
on his ice-cold forehead

Inflation

A bundle of bills
could buy
a flattering
smile
not long ago

Now
a bundle of bills
can buy
more than
one flattering
smile

Performers

The performing monkey
stretches out its hand
like a man
asking the spectators
for money

The performing man
stretches out his hand
like a monkey
asking the monkey
for money

Road

Twisting and turning
yet the road
constantly draws people
forward

It never thinks of itself
as the only right way
at every crossing
there's always a big sign pointing
TO WHAT TOWN
HOW MANY MILES

Under the Night Sky

A wolf
howling at the sky

smells
the bait
inside his fence

drops his tail
and becomes
a dog

Composition

If the sea gulls were not given a resting place
the sea would surely be lonely

And so the daring boats leave ports and sail
with their high masts

Old Woman

Like a worn-out record
the deep grooves
on her forehead
repeat and repeat

I want to live
I want to live
I want to

Spring Thunder

Waking me up
in the middle of the night
just to tell me
of his rumbling heart

Typhoon Season

Every year at this time
the woman within me
rages violently
with no provocation

And when it's over
I always hear her licking
my bleeding heart
with her tender tongue

Fall

a busy season
so many dreams
to sweep up

suddenly she rises
saying
it's time to go
then turns
and leaves

Autumn Leaves

Every leaf
helps
thicken
the carpet
&
soften
(
)
(
the
)
(
fall

Autumn Window

Now that she is middle-aged, my wife
likes to stand before the window
and comb her hair

Her only makeup a trace of cloud
the landscape of a graceful
poised maturity

Spring

If you wish to know
the shortest distance
between two woods
on this bright, enchanting day
any of the small, swift birds
can tell you with their twitter

It's not a straight line

Summer

Lofty season

A thick-plumed bird
on a branch
looks about perkily

Just as it should be
green, everything green

II.
Beyond
AUTUMN WINDOW

Song of Birth and Death

for a dying Somali child

He wants to blow up with his last breath
the collapsing balloons
that hang listlessly
from his mother's chest
and watch them soar
high into the sky

on this birthday of his
on this deathday of his

The Tree Under the Morning Sun

I laugh a thousand laughs
in the morning breeze
my whole body shakes and trembles
with joy

I know it's you dear
casting my shadow to the ground
your gaze burns my nape

Trees

trying to uphold something
trying to greet something
when the wind comes

but the clamors of the sixties are long gone
the protesting fists now tame as sheep

when the wind passes
the restless hands drop
become listless

Go-Go Dance

Shedding shedding shedding
your arms her hair my loneliness
Restless heels are red and swollen
the long journey of life is never ending

Desperate are the besieged souls
sallying forth at every beat of the war drums
and the horns are stretching their long necks
calling you calling you calling you
a string of ominous names

Darling
why are you shivering?

Midnight Mass

We then drove to the greenhouse
to see if the Cross was in bloom
the Cross that was planted 2000 years ago
the Cross that was once watered
with blood

When the pipe organ became the first one
to break down crying
we all picked up our coats and headed for the door
knowing it was another hopeless year

Only the stubborn caretaker refused to give up
he kept muttering something to himself
while sprinkling the air with water

Anxiety

The sea's hairy hands
are climbing up the mossy rocks
its malicious laughter, bouncing
between the disheveled wings of seagulls and the unshakable past
now splashing salty foam on your eyelids

I dare not write on the sand with my finger
lest you might remember
like recalling the ancient inscriptions
on a stone tablet

Autumn

puzzled by a falling leaf
he quietly put away
his guitar
and pictures of legs
in miniskirts

love it or leave it
What a choice

Evening Smokestack

frantically puffs
his pipe
under the dying sky
trying in vain
to make another ring
of smoke

A Woman

for a hat
she tempts men to kill
seven beautiful peacocks

in full pride

before seven mirrors
she chases joyfully
her own tail

Menarche

for a girl in a Chicago ghetto

Stumbling on a bumpy sidewalk
a little girl was hit by a stray bullet

Blood gushed from her immature body
Her stiffening mouth had yet to ask girlish questions
of her wailing mother

A Star-Studded World

Soap operas
of real people and real events
every day
from every corner of the earth
fight ferociously
for a bloody
Hollywood
shot

Spring

no good no good no good
shaking violently his head
the artist whitens his canvas
for a fresh start

tender green
just a tentative test stroke

Confucius Temple in Nanjing

Having learned the WAY in the morning,
it's quite all right to DIE that very evening.
—*Confucius*

Inside the dim temple
the starving Confucius says
Having learned the WAY in the morning
it's quite all right to DINE that very evening

Outside the temple
lights hanging over the eatery stalls
glitter with splendor
Crowds attracted by the aroma of food
pour in like ants

Masquerade

Walking in the streets
he suddenly realizes
last night's masquerade
is still going on

Everywhere he turns
he sees a mask
fastened to a face
like a second skin

April Fool's Day

April arrived
with a message on my desk
"Call Mr. Lyon—
Urgent!!!"

I dialed the number
"Sorry Mr. Lion can't come to the phone right now
He is in the CAGE!"
Before I could put down my phone
her irrepressible laugh jumped out of the line
and bit off my ear, splashing blood
all over my face

It then attacked my innocent officemate
I stood by helplessly and watched him
roll about and eventually die
of laughter

Canadian Rockies

Those unafraid of the cold
please step up

Immediately
the whole valley fills with pines
standing tall and erect

Lake Louise

so delicate
so vulnerable
in a chamber
deep in the high mountains

alone

there's got to be a sign
guarding
this little girl
of God

NO DINOSAURS ALLOWED
NO NOISY TOURISTS ALLOWED

Athabasca Falls

Maybe
this is the way
to deafen
the arrogant
ears
and pound straight
to the
heart

Deer X-ing

You can call me
a jaywalker if you like
but I must get to the other side
of your road
that divides our woods

When your overspeed rams
into my underestimate
you passionately kiss my bones
with your bumper
and I, in return, wash
your windshield
with my blood

Then you step on your gas
and are gone
while I gather all my might
for a final leap, trying in vain
to admire
for the last time, the brilliance
of the yellow sign

Silence

When poetic language
is used to ignite
hatred
and bombs
it's time to abandon
words
syllables
and sounds

To this absurd world
they really have nothing
to say

*Note: Many children born and raised in warring Bosnia were so traumatized
that they lost the ability to speak. Ironically, one of the Serbian leaders was
said to be a poet.*

Eclipse

Young at heart
the old sun
once in a while
likes to put on
his mischievous black mask
just to scare
the superstitious jittery
shadows

He doesn't know
we now keep shadows
safely in a world of virtual reality
where we eat and drink
make love
all without benefit
of a single ray
of sunlight

A Leap Second

With the Earth now rotating more slowly, the Central Bureau of the International Earth Rotation Service in Paris will add an extra "leap second" to the end of 1995.—Reuters, Dec. 18, 1995

Witnessing mother earth
stagger away at her advanced age
you stretch your farewell song
to the limit of your breath
and watch a man who is dead broke
laughing and crying
clutch in his hands
the windfall
of a long long
second

Social Event

From the sterile suburban life
to the drastic climate changes
they try desperately to find excuses
for a loud
burp

and he the originator
just stands there
nodding and smiling
as if nothing happened

Ghost Story

1

It is said
that even the most timid listener
survives

2

The candle flickers near the end of the story
shadows on the walls stretch then shrink
swaying right, left, back and forth
Together we move closer to each other
as the windows creak behind us
(are the ghosts too
moved by their own sad stories?)

Suddenly I am startled
by the touch of something...
a cold little hand

Winter Andante

In order to warm the eyes
white snow gently embraces
the naked trees and the fields

Distant mountains tremble softly
herds of deer with thickened hide
move slowly
in the vast empty woods

In the evening wind
the toll of a bell
quietly lights up the twinkling stars
adorning the sky
becoming a cathedral

Retirement

1

Finally
he can call
the clouds the birds the squirrels the flowers the trees
and millions of other things
by their first names
as now he too
is qualified for membership
in ANRB—
the Association of Never-Retired Beings

2

With a vacant step
he is surprised to find
under his feet
the exercise wheel
has turned
into level firm ground
where children after school
cheeringly scatter
to find new adventures

Born to Smile

—for Chelsey Thomas who was born unable to smile but after several operations, she was able to smile for the first time at her 8th birthday party.

In front of Life's big mirror
she has been practicing
for eight long years

just to show us
how to make
a hearty
smile

Mirror Lake

—Yosemite National Park

The mirror
dry and ragged
is made of stones

reflecting
the jutting face
of the sky

Sky Burial

1

At the Tibetan sky-burial site
the starting point
of reincarnation
they let his body soar
with his soul
piece by piece
to heaven

For the sake of the hooked beaks
of the circling vultures
which they believe to be
the Emissary of Death
they feverishly crush his stubborn skull
with a hammer
lest it should miss its last chance
and fall
into the everlasting deep

2

Huffing and puffing
they carried the corpse
of a poem
onto the sky-burial site
Without the touch of an ax or a knife
it fell to pieces by itself

Embalmed with aromatic oil
they tossed high into the sky
words and phrases
that were once beautiful and in good rhyme
hoping the Emissary of Death
would catch and take them
to heaven

Without even casting a glance
the vultures with their wings folded
just perched on the dead branches nearby
They had been taken in too many times
by such tasteless stuff
devoid of flesh and blood

Christmas Eve

a peaceful night

the gasping earth prays
for

a peaceful night

Installation Art

—for a visitor who has never seen snow before

Such a gigantic undertaking
needless to say is far beyond
the capability of an artist
like me

The snow on the grass
must be thick and soft and pure
tempting your innocent feet
to tread to sink to burst out laughing
The sun should make the icicles sparkle
in your dreaming eyes
and the breeze caressing your face
has to ripple your memory pond

On the top of Sears Tower
everything far and near
must be clear
The distant purple haze should not be
a blush of pollution but the flushed air
of this bustling city of steel

The floating ice on Lake Michigan needs to support

a flock of sun-bathing gulls
The tropical fish in the aquarium
should weave a colorful fairy tale
just for you

And of course
this masterful installation art
must be dismantled
right after you leave

Clone Songs

1

I love
you

I love
you you

I love
you you you you you you you you…

Would you please slow down a bit

2

With the same
clonal expression
a group of clones
solemnly gather
to witness the burial
of their original
dead of exhaustion

3

Ambitious politicians
will mass reproduce themselves
to gather votes

And once in power
they will without doubt eliminate
their blood replicas
knowing full well
that they are every cell
as power hungry
as themselves

Spring Snow

I know you love to dream

Standing in front of my window
I watch the snow
swirling in your dream
a sweet smile rippling
on your mouth

How I'd love to place an overseas call
raise the receiver towards the sky
and let you listen in your dream
to the sound of the snow
wafting and drifting

A Dreamless Night

From every angle
I tried to capture your bright smiles
for a colorful dream

Overexposed
the images overlapped
and I had a sweet dark sleep
till dawn

Temple

Only after its wooden roof has rotted
and collapsed
allowing the marble pillars to emerge
and prop up the sky
is the temple complete

A Midsummer Day's Dream

In his "Old Mistress Apologue," Franklin advises a friend to take an old mistress, saying, as in the dark all cats are grey, it is impossible of two women to know an old from a young one.

He holds her laziness in his hand
and plays with it for a long time
as if he is holding his favorite cat on his knee
stroking her silky fur

From a shadow in the glaring sun
suddenly words leap out
In the dark all cats are grey
which blind and hurt his eyes
He feels a pause
under his stroking hand
He then watches her take a long stretch
and with her half-closed eyes full of languor
her mouth slowly opens and is about to yawn
yet with the speed of a grey flash
she snatches at him and holds him in her mouth
like a rat

The Moonless Moon Festival

How do I know, tonight
above the heavy layers of dark clouds
the moon is a round ball, not a flat pancake
or a square or triangle block
or some formless mass
And how can I be sure
that there is only one moon
not a cluster
of man-made satellites

And of course in today's digital world
I can't rule out the possibility
of the old moon being now
a virtual image

Yet I know in my heart
that thousands of miles away
your gaze, penetrating the thick clouds
has filled the virtual image
with a pure brilliance
guiding my eyes
to the true moon

A Dark Horse

Not a single hair
is unbecoming
No particle of dust
clings to its polished eyes

If not for the glistening nose
and the rousing mane
you probably cannot tell
that it has just run all the way
from the depth
of a midnight dream

El Nino

Even God is weary
of the day-after-day
repetitions
and becomes a deconstructive
postmodernist

With a casual stir
the cradle
secure and stable
immediately goes
topsy-turvy

Morning Web

Every thread
flashes
the message of life
beautifully simple

while a fly
tries desperately
to decode
online

White House Sex Scandal

R-rated soap opera
red-faced
we are the audience
we are the supporting cast

Gravity

After thinking the matter through
the apple gracefully let itself
go

Oops
it landed right on the head
of Mr. Newton
dozing under the tree

Four Seasons

Spring

Such commotion
it can only be
first love

I don't recall ever seeing
so fresh a green

Summer

To say that your smile
lights up the whole garden
is of course an exaggeration

but I did indeed see
a flower bloom
at your approach

Autumn

Harvest season

not all flowers
need to bear
fruit

Winter

If not for the night's snow
how are the venturous feet to find
knee-deep shouts and laughter

or to look beyond
the vast white

A Dry Quiescent Afternoon

When wind comes
it brings hearsay of rain
and when rain comes
it brings hearsay of wind

And when you don't come
in this dry quiescent afternoon
I sit here and fabricate
all the hearsays
for the wind
and the rain

.

Scent

A short while ago
thousands of miles away
you were standing in the wind
facing me

Such keen sense
God bestows upon all animals
hungry
in cold dark nights

The Game of Blocks

It was right here
on this ruin of hearts
they built with their own hands
using sturdy colorful blocks
a magnificent lofty temple

As to what happened later
whether it was carelessly pushed over
by a bored hand
or one of the blocks
was so eroded by the elements
that it crumbled under its weight…
since it was such a long time ago
nobody could really tell

Carrying No Map, I Travel

In this land of beautiful scenery
there's no starting point
nor ending point

Hills, lakes, gentle slopes, unfathomable valleys
all try to lure my adventurous soul
into a perplexing maze

Under the tender strokes of hands
and exploring gaze
the water in the springs
the lava in the volcanoes
all rush to the surface in response
Come! Come!
Everywhere gates open with greeting arms

And to make sure I won't lose my way
you spread yourself like a roadmap
on the path of my life

A Mosquito's Ode to a Toad

With a soft moist tongue
you set up a sensuous trap
waiting for careless little me
to drop in

and be shocked
at the discovery
that I am such
a tasty prey

The Four-Sided Buddhist Idol in Macao

After she put together her palms
and offered a silent prayer on each side
she smiled at him shaking her head
secrets of heaven are not to be revealed

but he can tell from the duration and her facial expression
she has made four different wishes

Secretly he feels complacent
knowing the silent prayers he made on all sides
would have a fourfold chance of being fulfilled

Wishing her a boundless happiness
Wishing her a boundless happiness
Wishing her a boundless happiness
Wishing her a boundless happiness

A Fallen Goddess

He could not find the slightest crack
on the idol that he picked up from the floor
Wiping off the dust
he put it back in the high niche

Last night's earthquake
caused the downfall
that shook his faith

Now that all is well
no doubt he will go on with his worship

But the goddess who descended to earth last night
knows the man has failed her test
By repeatedly turning and inspecting
he has shattered her inner parts
irreparably

Two Suns or More

Finally came the news
the flesh and blood scattered
during the Big Bang
might have settled another solar system
44 light-years away

The possibility of having relatives
as cultured and peaceful as the human race
aroused intense excitement throughout the world
Now just let us pray
they and we worship
the same God

Smokestack

How shocking
the oversexed earth
still carries on
with such an erection

Between Heaven and Earth

A falling apple
suddenly stops midair
unsure of whether to continue its course
or return to the treetop
while the Kansas State Board of Education
argues over the weighty question
of gravity

A Drunk World

So much pent-up sorrow
so many beer cans popping
the world froths
and overflows

Aftershock

The bloody mutilated
terror
dug up from the ruins
by an excavator
still lies there
trembling

with intensity
exceeding the Richter scale
its epicenter
right in our heart

Cherokee Casino

A surviving band of Indians
finally settled
in the mountains near Cherokee

Using hunting skills handed down
from generation to generation
they built a trap with glittering lights
Now they just sit there and wait
for people of all colors
to drop in

Biltmore Mansion

Where can I find thousands of spacious buildings to house the
world's poor scholars and make them look happy
—Tu Fu, "Song of The Thatched Hut Blown Down by Autumn Wind"

This mansion, more spacious than a royal palace
might not be able to house all the world's poor scholars
but it can easily make a few hundred of them look
less unhappy

This morning the wind is calm and the sun bright
and these people holding tickets in their hands
with their heads high on their shoulders
sure don't look like any poor scholars to me
They move around the ornate furniture and decoration
admiring the beautiful image
of the hostess behind the curtains of time
and sniffing at the still-permeating aroma
of perfumed hair and wine and food
from banquets of a hundred years ago

Besides, they probably have never heard
of the name Tu Fu

In fact they might even confuse it
with Tofu, the weight-reducing health food
also from China

Biltmore House, the largest private home built in America at the end of the 19th century, is situated on 8,000 acres in Asheville, North Carolina. It has 250 rooms, 65 fireplaces, 43 bathrooms, 34 bedrooms, and 3 kitchens.

Cow & Cowhide

When a cow is flogged
with a cowhide

the pain must be bloody
immediate

Mona Lisa

There must be some d-e-e-p
secret

Staring at her smile
a man tilts his head left and right
Beside him a painted woman
wears a wide grin

Cezanne's Still Life

Lying back to back on a plate
an orange
and a banana
each dream
its own dream

Cezanne comes over
gives the banana
a half turn
Its graceful inner curve now
embraces the orange's plumpness

Instantly the air softens
the color fluid
and rich

Breath

A puff of air
from your sweet sigh
must have caused this breeze
that entices the flowers
to release their fragrance
and sends a shudder
through the leaves
and me

Spring Itch

Once again in his adolescence
the old tree in my backyard
keeps squeezing the budding acne
before the vanity mirror
of the blue sky

Super Lightspeed

A long time ago I discovered in you
the indubitable proof
of the existence of super lightspeed

You always knew
every word I was about to say
before I opened my mouth

Time Difference

It is morning
and he paces up and down the room
in silence

In a distant room
she too paces up and down
in silence
yet it is already evening

Thousands of miles apart
they walk to a window simultaneously
and look up at the half-lit sky
in silence

knowing at this moment
a flick of the eyelids or a twitch of the lips
will certainly set off
an avalanche

On the Towpath

Cut into the flesh
the rope
raw as original sin
pulls them back
on the muddy shore
each step a struggle
for the last stand

The endless succession of *ayo ayo*
is neither complaint
nor song
just to remind themselves
still alive

Bian-Zhong

An Ancient Chinese Musical Instrument Unearthed

They put in this time capsule
whispering wind from a bamboo grove
rippling stream under a wooden bridge
joyous shouts of children playing
gentle chat of grownups
mooing barking crowing chirping cooing
and the occasional rumbles
from a distant mountain

All of these and many more
they sealed and buried in the ground
to let us hear
thousands of years later
the ringing of a tranquil world

On the Viewing Stand of Tian An Men

From this height
all look so small
like ants

Except for the threatening clouds
and the guards
I might have raised both my arms
and proudly announced to the world
TODAY
I TOO
AM STANDING TALL

911

We really didn't care much about
the collapse of the Twin Towers
nor the Pentagon turning into a Tetragon
but when thousands of innocent lives
were agonizing in the flames
we frantically tried to dial for help
from Allah or whichever God

yet somehow we hesitated
there might not be anyone
on the other end

The Cove

With a sardonic laugh
the huge wave dashes toward her

She dodges
swaying slightly her hips

She then turns her head
and smiles

Immediately
the sea and sky become boundless
calm and tranquil

Bridge

Clasped together
intimate and tight

We really don't know
nor care
who was the first
to extend
a hand

Night Cruise on River Tuo

Dragon-Boat Festival, 2002

While our memory is still flickering and drifting
with the water lamps in the stream of time
our eyes are already filled with fog
like the chilly surface of tonight's river

The drumbeats pounding our chests all day
are finally silent
waves stirred up by thousands of paddles
have also calmed

Under the hazy starlight
a couple of mandarin ducks
are chattering and necking

don't forget tonight

Jade Necklace

A live cinder
from the Creation

Stroking with your finger tips
you stir up the green flame
that flickers on your breast
then smile
and walk straight towards me

Listening to a Childhood Song

Flickering across the dark open space
a firefly...
then two...
then three...
soon they multiply
become flashes of lightning
reveal ragged hills
and mountains
overflowing rivers
and ravines
of a face

Neighbor's Flowers

A week ago our neighbor Eddie passed away
This morning I saw the potted flowers on their patio
all drooped and withered

His wife Helen who loves flowers so much
must not have heard the weather report
warning of an early frost

Transmigration

Swaying alone in the evening wind
a little blue flower in the wilderness

a passing poet with misty eyes
suddenly turns his head
and gazes upon her

One evening centuries later
a faded blue book of poetry
stands at the corner of a dusty bookshelf

a little blue flower in the wilderness
swaying alone in the evening wind

Songs of You and Me

1

I let
the bird
in your cage
go

I know you want
to hear him
sing

but I believe
the acoustics are much better
in the woods

2

I put out
your lamp

It was kind of you
to try to illuminate
the way
for the moths

but I believe they can see
far better
in the dark

3

I snatch the sweet dream
from a smiling corner
of your mouth

You turn over
murmuring something
strange yet familiar

It turns out to be
my long lost
childhood name

Someone Must Be Crying

for Iris Chang

Someone must be crying
in such an evening
wind coming from the west
rain coming from the west

and she is the one
who can't hold her tears
after seeing so many piles
of white bones in history
the injustice and the dead silence
of the world

and she is the one
who once starts crying
cannot stop
human sins surround her like icebergs
choke her
with their oppressive shadows

Someone must be crying
in such an evening
wind coming from the west
rain coming from the west

*Iris Chang was a Chinese-American writer who in 1997
published a book entitled "The Rape of Nanking: The Forgotten
Holocaust of World War II" telling the story of the murder of
more than 250,000 defenseless civilians by the invading Japanese
army. In 2004 she committed suicide due to severe depression.

Tsunami Time

When acres and acres of debris
can no longer be used
to reconstruct the memories
of sunshine and laughter

When a bloated body becomes
the last hope and comfort
to grief-stricken relatives
survival is not an option but a miracle

When black tidal waves crash down
one after another in our nightmares
we scream helplessly
and wake up soaking wet

When all fishermen suffer from hydrophobia
a lone boy picks up a stone
and throws it toward the sea
with all his might

When people around the world
no matter where they are
instantly become
orphans

Melting Icicles

at the mere sight
of the sun's warm smile
the frozen tears
of the lovelorn
winter
begin to
melt
and
d
r
i
p

At the Laundromat

a laundry bag
stuffed
with smelly
days
of the gone week

he begins his ritual—
emptying contents into the washer
adding bleach
and detergent
closing the lid
putting three coins in the slots

the recycle
of another week

Have a Hammock

The Maya still sleep in hammocks
between two trees. "Have a hammock"
is their daily greeting

Bright sunshine above
cool grass below
swinging between two trees
a sweet Mayan dream

Dark sky above
a sea of lights below
swinging between two skyscrapers
an acrophobe's nightmare

Newborn

The world
is full of
light and smiles

Light and smiles
are the things he sees
when opening his eyes
the very first time

Bird Fish Poet

Getting lost
in the smoky sky
a bird asks a cloud
for direction

In the water
where no sunlight can penetrate
a bubbling fish desperately seeks
its own shadow

A poet strolls the brown earth
looking casually up and down
now at the bird now at the fish
finally finds his inspiration
and composes a beautiful poem

Katrina

With such a name
of course she had to be
a wild dancer

A slight swing of her wide skirt
instantly sent all watchers
into a daze
not able to escape
nor to tell
if what engulfed the city
was water from the ruptured levees
or tears from their eyes

On the turbid water's surface
there were bloated bodies
querying the sky
with outstretched arms

Endangered Species

He can't recall
when he became
an endangered species

yet he can sense
the pitying stares
behind the scopes
streaming towards him
like bullets

flying alone
in the vast vast sky
he knows he must utter
his last cry

like a poet
who sings
to confirm his being

An Easter Surprise

Lying magnificently in the nest
the two blue eggs, still radiant
with the mother's warmth
must have been hidden by God
to give children an Easter surprise
yet I, no longer a child
happen to find them

The mother bird startled away
by my intrusion
is now standing on the grass
watching my every move

Though knowing well
the briefer a beauty is
the more lasting it can become
I still want another look
but promise to let the mother
get back to her nest
before her warmth on the eggs
dissipates completely

Jewish Cemetery in Budapest

Unwilling to be forgotten
the memories of humanity
rather inhumanity
struggle hard
to emerge
from layers beneath layers

tombstones
aslant and askew

A Helicopter Upside Down in a Public Place

To fly from this position
is of course difficult
unless
we too stand on our heads
and rapidly cross our feet

Sure enough
we hear the propeller starting to roar
yippeeeeee
and we soar high into the sky
above the cheering crowd

5/27/2006 8:06 pm
cold rain falling hard
at the Residentsplatz

not a single soul in sight

* As part of Mozart's 250th birthday celebration activities in
Salzburg, A Helicopter Upside Down In A Public Place" was an
art piece displayed at the Residentsplatz. The artist, Paola Pivi,
was born in Milan in 1971. Her works are enigmatic, patently
absurd and humorous. When displayed in public spaces, her
creations are meant to surprise and amuse viewers, lifting them
briefly from their ordinary routine.

The Transmigration of a Humorist

Hi. I am Art Buchwald
and I just died

no sooner had he finished his words
than I heard a baby's cry

Hi. I am Art Buchwald
and I was just born

Winter Palaces Summer Palaces Big Palaces Small Palaces

Russian Impression #1

Hoisted to the sky
a magnificent dome

My upward-looking eyes
suddenly become blurred
as drops of sweat and blood
flying through the dim air of history
splatter my face

Toilet Reality

Russian Impression #2

It took only a few days
for him to get used to the grandiose dreams
of Imperial Russia
the imposing columns
the onion domes
the magnificent churches
the even more magnificent palaces
the biggest cannon the heaviest bell the tallest statue
and in the five-star hotel
the insurmountable bathtub
the elevated toilet...

In fact it was the homely American toilet
that plunged him back
to earth

Mountain Views

At Dawn

You have never seen
such a fresh world
rising from bird songs
in such a fine morning

every ray of light
brilliant and dazzling
each love
the first love

At Dusk

Without the tick of the second hand
or chirp of birds
without the changing light moving across the window sill
or footsteps of the wind rustling the leaves
I might not have become aware of the darkening twilight
permeating the corner of your eyes

A rude hand
carrying a heavy shadow
is slowly approaching
your proud and defiant forehead

A Butterfly Specimen

netted with one scoop

dazzling wings
bright sunshine
gentle breeze
flower fragrance
soft birdsong
fluid glances

now a Latin name
in the dim light
of the museum

Fairy Penguin Parade

A night on Phillip Island, Australia

1

In complete silence
they march in file onto the stage
like well-rehearsed kindergarteners
their white-breasted costumes
glittering joyously
under the dim light

Since no flash is allowed
it is hard to tell
from which backstage they emerge
the boundless ocean
or the dark night

In wobbling steps
without any gesture
or dialogue
they shake water off their bodies
and fill the eyes of the audience
with tears

2

Exultant over their freedom
they have again spent all day in the Ocean Bar
celebrating and drinking
and now pop ashore
one by one

Oblivious to all furtive eyes in the dark
they form a line on the beach
and do their routine exercises
left....right...left.........right
trying strenuously to turn their unsteady steps
into graceful movements of the waves
before they reach home

Recollection Tricks

after sixty years

Raising his foot
he stepped right into the magnificent palace
where he was once a happy little prince

Surprised
he found the tall threshold
had shrunk and sunk
and he suddenly became a giant
trapped in a miniature room
with crumbling walls

Above the courtyard
the ever bright vast sky of his memory
was now downcast
with sunken shoulders
and eyes staring blankly
at his perplexed look

Curves

an enticing glance
the profile of a body
lying on its side

lips parting slightly
a dialogue
between
two distant stars

Sea O Sea

Slaughtering pilot whales in the Faroe Islands, Denmark

Calm after carnage
the bloody sea
finally ceases boiling

Soon the night curtain will fall
to conceal the savage scene
letting the glaring red fade
into the deep dark corner
of unhumankind's memory

Sydney Opera House

full sails
outspread wings
ready to dispatch
every note
to eager ears

lights dim
silently they wait
for the baton to rise
and summon music
from some mysterious corner
of the universe

Snowstorm

bury deep
every unseasonable
passion

then invite adventurous feet
to trample
scribble nonsense

About the Author

William Marr has published, under the Chinese pen name Fei Ma, fourteen books of poetry in his native Chinese language. His first book of poems in English, *Autumn Window*, was published by Arbor Hill Press (1995, and 2nd Edition 1996). His poems appear in numerous anthologies including *300 Best New Poems 1917-1995*, published in Taiwan, and *300 Best Chinese New Poems*, published in China and are widely read in Taiwan, China, Hong Kong, Southeast Asia, and the United States. His works are included in high school and college textbooks of Chinese Literature in Taiwan and China. A number of his poems have been translated into many languages. In addition to writing poetry, he has also edited several anthologies of Chinese and Taiwanese modern poetry. A former president of the Illinois State Poetry Society and a member of the Poets Club of Chicago, he is a scientist by profession and has lived and worked in the Chicago area since 1970.

* * *

Bill Marr is a fellow painter, poet, and all-round great fellow. We met in the '80s before he retired from Argonne National Laboratory in Chicago. With more time to pursue his writing, he soon became the second president of the Illinois State Poetry Society and also joined the Poets Club of Chicago. His poems, always short, sharp and well-aimed, intrigued me early on. Never one to milk his subjects, he goes straight to the heart of his topics and his readers, making his work unforgettable. As in KATRINA and MENARCHE he deals with tragedy both poignantly and succinctly but with keen insight. His wife, Jane, has inspired tender and memorable poems such as AUTUMN WINDOW and SHARING AN UMBRELLA. Marr's work is well-known in China, Taiwan and Southeast Asia and he has translated much of his and other writers' works into Chinese. In addition to publishing fourteen books of his own poetry here and abroad, he has edited a number of Chinese and Taiwanese contemporary works. After coming to the U.S.A. in 1961 and receiving a Ph.D. in Nuclear Engineering from the University of Wisconsin in 1969, Bill Marr settled into an American lifestyle, but he never lost the incisive Oriental perspective that defines his poetry and makes it unique.—Glenna Holloway, founding president of Illinois State Poetry Society, author of **NEVER FAR FROM WATER and OTHER LOVE STORIES**

When viewing the world as a nuclear physicist and poet, how do the particles of perception intermix, and what does perception say of our world among the stars? The atomic forces, the halos, that surround all objects animate and inanimate inter-relate across boundaries of life, time, and history. The Yellow River of China flows seaward upon the eyes of those who have farmed its banks and wasted its waters upon their lives and land, indeed from those from whom it has sucked its sustenance. The artist, awake as never before to his painting, leaves the easel only to have his work completed by a wandering stranger. Flickering across darkness, a firefly becomes flashes of lightning that reveal hills, mountains, rivers, and the ravines of a human face. An ancient flute lifted from the earth whistles only the sounds of a forgotten time that haunts our bones. No dust clings to the eye of the dark horse which has run all the way from a night dream. A woman snatches at a man and holds him in her mouth like a rat. And only after the wooden roof of a temple has rotted and collapsed are its pillars able to emerge and prop up the sky—the temple complete. Between Heaven and Earth is the second book of poetry in English by renowned Taiwanese poet Fei Ma, or as his friends at Argonne National Lab know him, William Marr. (He has written 14 volumes of poetry in his native Chinese.) They are the poems of a man who travels widely, observes deeply and speaks sparsely, for there is so much of the world to look at, and it is the fractal patterns of the world—the spaces between the rough edges of being and non-being that must be looked at and experienced for our lives to have human definition in the open echoing of the stars from which we are born.—Jared Smith, author of **Grassroots** and **The Graves Grow Bigger Between Generations**

Some Comments on the Author's Previous Works

Verse has never been freer, yet strong discipline is at work...The human spectrum visible in *Autumn Window* will make readers nod, smile and perhaps wipe an eye.—*Chicago Tribune*

Collectible Chicago poets, one finds, start with Eugene Field, Carl Sandburg, Edgar Lee Masters, Harriet Monroe, Gwendolyn Brooks, Ana Castillo, David Hernandez, Li-Young Lee, William Wei-Yi Marr, and a raft of more recent poets...—*AB Bookman's Weekly, For The Specialist Book World*

He uses fluently and clearly the language of the common people...gives profound meaning to common objects and events.—*The Isle Full of Noises, Modern Chinese Poetry from Taiwan*, Columbia University Press

Unquestionably among the best contemporary Chinese poets...He is unique and without peer in the arena of short poems.—*Huaxia Poetry* (China)

A master of lyrical layers along with the beauty and brevity of his Chinese heritage, he enhances his skill with the spontaneity and flavor of his adopted American homeland. His humor, insight and tenderness are universal; his control of such rich ingredients is sure-handed.—Glenna Holloway

Each (poem) is a window opening onto beauty and fluency. There is every shade of happiness and sadness, anger and peace...Their effortless renderings of a civilized mind in touch with an often mad world are part of their mystery.—Li-Young Lee

His concise yet highly symbolic poetry, with a deep sense of humanity, adds a new dimension to the rich tradition of Chinese poetry...He bridges the gap between new and old, and between East and West.—*Hong Kong Literature Monthly*